EDITED BY HELEN EXLEY

Published in 2019 by Helen Exley®LONDON in Great Britain.
Illustration by Juliette Clarke © Helen Exley Creative Ltd 2019.
All the words by Charlotte Gray, Odile Dormeuil, Linda Macfarlane,
Stuart & Linda MacFarlane, Helen Exley, Helen Thomson, Dalton
Exley, Mathilde & Sebastien Forestier, Harry Altdon and Amanda Bell
copyright © Helen Exley Creative Ltd 2019.
Design, selection and arrangement © Helen Exley Creative Ltd 2019.
The moral right of the author has been asserted.

ISBN 978-1-78485-226-9

12 11 10 9 8 7 6 5 4 3 2 1

OTHER BOOKS IN THE SERIES

Be Happy!   *Be Confident!*   *Be Brave!*
Be a Rebel!   *Be You!*

OTHER BOOKS BY HELEN EXLEY

365 Yes to life!   365 Happy Days!   Mindful Days...365

The little book of Gratitude   The book of Positive Thoughts

Helen Exley®LONDON,
16 Chalk Hill, Watford, Herts WD19 4BG, UK
www.helenexley.com

Be Positive!

Helen Exley

*Start where you are.
Use what you have.
Do what you can.*

ARTHUR ASHE

Keep your thoughts positive because your thoughts become your words.

Keep your words positive because your words become your behaviour.

Keep your behaviour positive because your behaviour becomes your habits.

Keep your habits positive because your habits become your values.

Keep your values positive because your values become your destiny.

MAHATMA GANDHI

May your choices reflect your hopes, not your fears.

NELSON ROLIHLAHLA MANDELA

You can have anything you want
if you want it desperately enough.
You must want it with an exuberance
that erupts through the skin
and joins the energy that created
the world.

SHEILA GRAHAM

You have to trust
in something –
your gut, destiny,
life, karma,
whatever...

STEVE JOBS

Why not just live in the moment, especially if it has a good beat?

GOLDIE HAWN

Some days there won't be a song in your heart. Sing anyway.

EMORY AUSTIN

Be positive.
Have only positivity
going through your body.
Be the best.
Being the best starts by acting
Like U R the best.
Believing U R the best.
Becoming the best.
Believe.
Become.

SERENA WILLIAMS

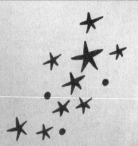

Shoot for the moon.
Even if you miss,
you'll land
among the stars.

NORMAN VINCENT PEALE

Live your Joy,
Go against the grain.
Let nature's curious wisdom fill you.
Let the world's mystical heritage
guide you.
Paint your canvases,
play your tunes.

SIR THOMAS MORE

Have a Rainbow Day –
enjoy every colour and shade
of happiness.

LINDA GIBSON

Change your habits totally.
In everything you do
give up negativity, thank people,
laugh, give compliments.
Every day, every hour,
Smile. Smile. Smile.

DALTON EXLEY

To be happy, drop the words
"if only" and substitute instead
the words "next time."

DR. SMILEY BLANTON

For people sometimes believed
that it was safer to live with complaints,
was necessary to cooperate with grief,
was all right to become
an accomplice in self-ambush...
Take heart to flat out decide
to be well and stride
into the future sane and whole.

TONI CADE BAMBARA

Oppose a negative
wave of thought with
a positive wave
of thought.

GAUTAMA BUDDHA

If opportunity doesn't knoc

Keep on looking for the bright,
bright skies;
Keep on hoping that the sun will rise;
Keep on singing
when the whole world sighs,
And you'll get there in the morning.

HENRY HARRY THACKER BURLEIGH

uild a door. MILTON BERLE

Everyone in this world has a gift.
Find it. Encourage it.
Astonish yourself.

PAM BROWN

Always end the day
with a positive thought,
no matter how hard
things were.
Tomorrow's a fresh
opportunity
to make it better.

AUTHOR UNKNOWN

I am only one,
But still I am one.
I cannot do everything,
But still I can do
something;
And because I cannot
do everything
I will not refuse
to do the something
that I can do.

EDWARD EVERETT HALE

Be glad.
Life is so rare a gift in this
vast universe
that any price is worth
the paying.
To live is to have been given
treasures beyond belief.

CHARLOTTE GRAY

Live your life each day as you would
climb a mountain. An occasional glance
toward the summit keeps the goal in mind,
but many beautiful scenes
are to be observed from each new
vantage point. Climb slowly, steadily,
enjoying each passing moment,
and the view from the summit
will service as a fitting climax
for the journey.

HAROLD V. MELCHERT

Life engenders life.
Energy creates energy.
It is by spending oneself
that one becomes rich.

SARAH BERNHARDT

Never give up

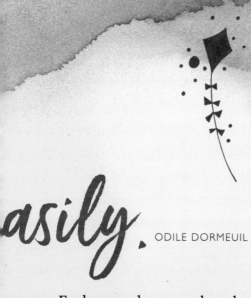

asily. ODILE DORMEUIL

Each second you can be reborn.
Each second there can be a new beginning.
It is choice, it is your choice.

CLEARWATER

To be aged
to perfection and happy.
To dance.
To run.
To walk for miles along the shore.
To sing.
Gather it up.
Store it like honey
to shine with a golden light,
to bring a sweetness
to your whole life.

CHARLOTTE GRAY

Write the bad things
that are done to you
in sand, but write
the good things
that happen to you
on a piece of marble.

ARAB PROVERB

Don't look
at your feet
to see if you
are doing it right.
Just dance.

ANNE LAMOTT

The warrior of life
is a believer.
Because we believe
in miracles,
miracles begin to happen.
Because we believe
our thoughts
can change our life,
our life begins to change.

PAULO COELHO

Stay positive.
Be happy.
Live free.

AUTHOR UNKNOWN

** ***

Just think of the negativity-world
as an enemy whose strength
can be weakened by your smile.

SRI CHINMOY

Be one of those
special people –
the ones who encourage others.
The ones who are always
enthusiastic.

DALTON EXLEY

Here in your hand
you hold the world.
Marvels once only known
to scholars,
travellers, the rich.
People and places.
Galleries, museums, palaces.
Speculations and discoveries.
Take what you need.
And use it well.

CHARLOTTE GRAY

Validate yourself,
your abilities,
your gifts,
your understandings.
Validate your
uniqueness...

BLACKWOLF (ROBERT JONES),
OJIBWE, AND GINA JONES

You must learn day by day,
year by year,
to broaden your horizon.
The more things you love,
the more you are interested in,
the more you enjoy,
the more you are
indignant about –
the more you have left
when anything happens.

ETHEL BARRYMORE

Nothing great
was ever achieved
without enthusiasm.
The way of life
is wonderful;
it is by abandonment.

RALPH WALDO EMERSON

A problem is a chanc

Success is a state of mind.
If you want success, start thinking
of yourself as a success.

DR. JOYCE BROTHERS

or you to do your best.

DUKE ELLINGTON

If you want to build bridges
use bolts and girders –
if you want to build
your future
use hope and determination.

STUART & LINDA MACFARLANE

Hope's such a wonderful thing!
Helping humanity through the ages,
now and into the future.
Bright hope shines within all of us.
Believe in it, believe in yourself,
believe in today,
believe in tomorrow
and believe in the future.
Let's all help make it
what we dream and hope for.

HARRY ALTDON

If you think you can,
you can.

MARY KAY ASH

Hope, tomorrow
and tomorrow still,
And every tomorrow hope;
trust while you live.

VICTOR HUGO

May you never cease
to search and challenge.
May you always find
something to delight you.
May you always
have joy in living.

PAM BROWN

L**ive all you can;**
it's a mistake not to.
It doesn't so much matter
what you do in particular
so long as you
have your life.

HENRY JAMES

Perpetual optimism is

When life gives a hundred reasons
to break down and cry, show life
that you have a thousand reasons
to smile and laugh. Stay Strong.

AUTHOR UNKNOWN

rce multiplier. COLIN L. POWELL

Never look down to test the ground
before taking your next step:
only they who keep their eyes
fixed on the far horizon
will find the right road.

DAG HAMMARSKJÖLD

It begins with the vision
to recognize when a job,
a life stage, a relationship, is over –
and let it go.
It involves a sense of the future,
a belief that every exit line
is an entry,
that we are moving on,
rather than out.

ELLEN GOODMAN

After the rain
the grass will shed its moisture,
the fog will lift from the trees,
a new light will brighten the sky
and play in the drops
that hang on all things.
Your heart will beat out
a new gladness,
– if you let it happen.

CHIEF DAN GEORGE, COAST SALISH

Hope begins in the dark, the stubborn
hope that if you just show up and try
to do the right thing, the dawn will come.
You wait and watch and work:
you don't give up.

ANNE LAMOTT

Fall seven times

No matter how dark the cloud,
there is always a thin,
silver lining, and that is what
we must look for.
The silver lining will come…

WANGARI MAATHAI

Stand up eight.

JAPANESE PROVERB

A new life begins for us
with every second.
Let us go forward joyously to meet it.
We must press on,
whether we will or no,
and we shall walk better
with our eyes before us
than with them ever cast behind.

JEROME K. JEROME

May you find happiness
everywhere you turn.
In love and friendship.
In music, theatre, art.
In mountains, oceans, deserts.
In woods and rivers.
In taste and scent and sound.

CHARLOTTE GRAY

Think of all the beauty
that's still left
in and around you
and be happy!

ANNE FRANK

Live for the hope
of good things to come,
not only here and now,
but in generations to follow.

BEAR HEART (MUSKOGEE)

Hold your head high,
stick your chest out.
You can make it.
It gets dark sometimes
but morning comes...

JESSE JACKSON

Positivity, happiness, kindness and smiles are infectious! Start an outbreak!

DALTON EXLEY

I think that you must try.
You have to try to be nice, try to be
positive, try to make a go of things.
Try to make a party a good one,
try to say thank you for everything
you've got and be grateful to people.
Don't just sit back and expect
things to happen.

JOANNA LUMLEY

Wear your dreams like diamonds.

LINDA GIBSON

Part of being optimistic
is keeping one's head
pointed toward the sun,
one's feet moving forward.

NELSON ROLIHLAHLA MANDELA

This moment of your life is special –
unique. Do not burden it
with regrets of the past
or making plans for some vague,
distant future.
Live this moment.
Enjoy it.
It is your moment.
Love it.
Live it.

LINDA MACFARLANE

When one door closes another opens.
Expect that new door
to reveal even greater wonders
and glories and surprises.
Feel yourself grow
with every experience.
And look for the reason for it.

EILEEN CADDY

*Never look back
unless you are planning
to go that way.*

HENRY DAVID THOREAU

You're braver than you believe,
and stronger than you seem,
and smarter than you think.

A. A. MILNE

Twenty years from now you
will be more disappointed
by the things that you didn't do
than the ones you did do.
So throw off the bowlines.
Sail away from safe harbor.
Catch the trade winds
in your sails.
Explore. Dream. Discover.

MARK TWAIN

Dream.
Dream
yourself free.

STUART & LINDA MACFARLANE

Let your body tell you
you're powerful and deserving,
and you become more present,
enthusiastic and authentically yourself.

AMY CUDDY

Enthusiasm is the mo

eautiful word on earth.

CHRISTIAN MORGENSTERN

Don't look back and ask why.
Look ahead and demand "Why not!"

AUTHOR UNKNOWN

In the theatre of life
you are the director,
the choreographer and
the lead actor.
The stage is yours;
dance in the spotlight,
sing to the crowds,
give a stunning performance.

MATHILDE & SÉBASTIEN FORESTIER

The beauty of new fallen snow
is that you can create your own
unique path upon it –
a path along which others
may well follow.
The future is a field of snow.
Plough your own path;
make it one that others
will be proud to follow.

LINDA GIBSON

Your success and happiness
lie in you. External conditions
are the accidents of life.
Resolve to keep happy,
and your joy and you shall form
an invincible host against difficulty.

HELEN KELLER
(BORN BOTH DEAF AND BLIND)

Each time one of us stands up
for an ideal or acts to improve the lot
of others, or strikes out against injustice,
we send out a ripple of hope, and crossing
each other from a million centres
of energy and daring, those ripples build
a current that can sweep down
the mightiest walls of oppression
and resistance.

ROBERT F. KENNEDY JR.

*If you can change your mind,
you can change your life.*

WILLIAM JAMES

* * * * *

You must make a decision that you are going to move on. It won't happen automatically. You will have to rise up and say, "I don't care how hard this is, I don't care how disappointed I am, I'm not going to let this get the best of me. I'm moving on with my life."

JOEL OSTEEN

I live by one principle: Enjoy life with no conditions! People say, "If I had your health, if I had your money, oh, I would enjoy myself." It is not true. I would be happy if I were lying sick in a hospital bed. It must come from the inside. That is the one thing I hope to have contributed to my children, by example and by talk: to make no conditions, to understand that life is a wonderful thing and to enjoy it, every day, to the full.

ARTHUR RUBINSTEIN

Each day is a gift.

Open it.

Celebrate.

Enjoy it.

STUART & LINDA MACFARLANE

…there are times
when I think to myself
how wonderful life can be!
Believe me, it's true!
So stop what you're doing
this minute and get happy.
Work at making yourself happy!

HARUKI MURAKAMI

What were the odds of you
ever coming into existence?
A trillion never made it.
Treasure this extraordinary gift.
Delight in the wonders
chance has given you.

PAM BROWN

Jump into the middle of things,
get your hands dirty,
fall flat on your face, and
then reach for the stars.

JOAN L. CURCIO

It does not matter how long
you are spending on the earth,
how much money you have
gathered or how much attention
you have received.
It is the amount of positive vibration
you have radiated in life that matters.

AMIT RAY

Every day must come to you
as a new hope, a new promise,
a new aspiration.
Every day you have to energize
yourself anew.
For it is only with newness
that you can succeed
and transcend yourself.

SRI CHINMOY

*Whatever you attempt,
go at it with spirit.
Put some in!*

DAVID STARR JORDAN

There are certain things
that our age needs. It needs, above all,
courageous hope and the impulse
to creativeness.

BERTRAND RUSSELL

Whatever you can do or dream you can.
Begin it.
Boldness has genius, magic and power in it.
Begin it now.

JOHANN WOLFGANG VON GOETHE

Don't ever dream big,
dream huge, and then
you'll achieve big.

MIKO RWAYITARE

…from the sky, from the earth,
from a scrap of paper,
from a passing shape,
from a spider's web…
We must pick out what is good for us
where we can find it.

PABLO PICASSO

Give every day the chance to become the most beautiful of your life.

MARK TWAIN

Enthusiasm is the yeast that makes
your hopes rise to the stars.
Enthusiasm is the sparkle in your eyes,
the swing in your gait,
the grip of your hand,
the irresistible surge of will and energy
to excite your ideas.

HENRY TOR

My will shall shape my future.
Whether I fail or succeed shall be
no man's doing but my own.
I am the force; I can clear any
obstacle before me or I can be lost
in the maze. My choice;
my responsibility;
win or lose, only I hold the key
to my destiny.

ELAINE MAXWELL

Be realistic.
Plan for a miracle.

BHAGWAN SHREE RAJNEESH

You have to accept whatever comes
and the only important thing
is that you meet it with courage
and the best you have to give.

ELEANOR ROOSEVELT

Let happiness astonish you. Open your arms to life.

PAM BROWN

This is your shining hour –
all the glory
of the universe is yours.

ODILE DORMEUIL

Before you begin a thing remind
yourself that difficulties and delays
quite impossible to foresee are ahead...
You can only see one thing clearly,
and that is your goal.
Form a mental vision of that
and cling to it through thick and thin.

KATHLEEN THOMPSON NORRIS

Throw your heart
out in front of you
And run ahead
to catch it.

ARAB PROVERB

All our dreams can come true –
if we have the courage to pursue them.

WALT DISNEY

Believe in hope,
grow into hope,
and breathe in at every moment
the fragrance and beauty of hope.

SRI CHINMOY

Find new projects, more
friends, more love.
Say "Yes" to it all.

HELEN EXLEY

Separate yourself from those
who hinder your vision.
Make a choice to walk away from
the trap set to ensnare you.
Realize when someone is pulling you
backwards every time you take
a step forward. Separate from them
and the result of your action
will be a life of success.

AMAKA IMANI NKOSAZANA

There is not one day
of your life
that is worth

wasting being sad.
Be Happy!!

MATHILDE & SÉBASTIEN FORESTIER

*Find what fills you,
what enlivens you...
what you love.*

SUSAN SQUELLATI FLORENCE

Keep a green tree in our heart
and perhaps a singing bird will come.

CHINESE PROVERB

There are two ways to look at mountains;
something frightening, too difficult
a challenge to take on or a beautiful
feature on the landscape of life
to observe, to climb and enjoy.
Each day we have mountains
in our lives – rise to the challenge
of each and celebrate
every single achievement.

STUART & LINDA MACFARLANE

When your bow is broken
and your last arrow spent, then shoot,
shoot with your whole heart.

ZEN SAYING

Never run ou

Sing! Dance! Laugh!
Be positive!

HELEN EXLEY

of goals. EARL NIGHTINGALE

We must free ourselves in the hope
that the sea will ever rest.
We must learn to sail in high winds.

ARISTOTLE ONASSIS

There are really only two ways
to approach life: as victim or as
gallant fighter.
You must decide if you want to
act or react.
Deal your own cards or play
with a stacked deck.
And if you don't decide which way
to play with life,
it always plays with you.

MERLE SHAIN

Five things to declare daily:

1. I am amazing.
2. I can do anything.
3. Positivity is a choice.
4. I celebrate my individuality.
5. I am prepared to succeed.

Our actions, which are driven by our feelings, offer us the opportunity to live; they let us go out and leave a mark... Actions cause things to happen and from those outcomes we learn, we improve and we find the best path for an amazing existence. We make our own masterpiece. And it all starts from a blank canvas.

JONNY WILKINSON

When you believe in something you create a pathway for receiving it. If you believe life is great, you see great possibilities, you plan for them and, through your actions, you produce them. If you are doubtful and fearful, you shun opportunities, you limp through life, and everything you touch turns to dust.

SUSAN L. TAYLOR

May you always find new projects,
new friends, new love.
May you always find new paths to wander,
new adventures to dare, new chapters
of life to open, new changes
to challenge you.

HELEN EXLEY

Aim for the moon.
If you miss, you may hit a star.

W. CLEMENT STONE

A great attitude
becomes a great day
which becomes a great month
which becomes a great year
which becomes a great life.

MANDY HALE